Encyclopedia of Animals

for Young Readers

Albatros

CONTENTS

MAMMALS

This diverse group of animals includes not only humans, but also mice and elephants. Mammals have one thing in common: we all drink breast milk after we're born. The milk gives us all the nutrients we need to grow, as well as the necessary energy to keep our body temperature constant. Most mammals have fur. However, this doesn't apply to everybody. For example, dolphins and whales may look like fish but are actually mammals. Their bodies have adapted perfectly to the water environment. The young of many mammals are born relatively developed and can move independently. One exception is marsupials, whose offspring must first grow up a bit in their mom's pouch.

✳ European hare

The young of the European hare spend only a couple of weeks in a burrowed nest where their mom breastfeeds them before they're forced to stand up on their own feet.

✳ Red fox

As canines and predators, foxes are skilled hunters. But they're no picky eaters. When a fox is hungry, it doesn't say no to earthworms, beetles, or some fruit. Its curiosity often brings it all the way to human settlements.

✳ Platypus

When this animal was first discovered, scientists thought it was some kind of joke. The platypus has a beak, four legs with a membrane between its toes, and a hairy body—and to top it all off, it lays eggs!

Platypus

European hare

Koala

Red fox

Amazon river dolphin

Large flying fox

5

✳ Koala

The easygoing koala doesn't bother finding a nest or burrow for its offspring. After birth, the tiny baby hides in its mom's belly pouch, where it feeds on her milk.

✳ Amazon river dolphin

Dolphins have adapted to living in the water so well that they look like fish. But they're actually mammals, just like us. They feed their offspring breast milk and have to come to the surface to breathe.

✳ Large flying fox

Some mammals are even capable of flying. The best-known chiropterans include flying foxes and bats. In the case of large flying foxes, their wingspan can be nearly five feet.

Rodents

What will we sink our teeth into?

They live in diverse environments, aren't very large, and like to have a bit to eat. Their super-sharp teeth can get through all sorts of things—very useful when you need to burrow a den, or even fell a tree.

Crested porcupine

Common hamster

Red squirrel

Naked mole rat

Alpine marmot

✳ Naked mole rat

Naked mole rats aren't exactly known for having shaggy fur. They bite their way through narrow underground tunnels, breathe slowly, and their naked skin can't feel pain. Additionally, they live remarkably long lives.

✳ Red squirrel

Squirrels are excellent tree climbers and can jump from one branch to another without making a single error. They build their dens in tree hollows.

✳ Brown rat

When humans started to develop water transport, this curious rodent—skilled both on dry land and in water—spread throughout the world. Albino laboratory rats, on the other hand, were bred by humans.

✳ Crested porcupine

Porcupines aren't exactly fans of running, which is why they rely on their sharp quills when in danger—they bristle up and turn the quills toward the attacker.

✳ Alpine marmot

Most marmots live in burrow-dwelling colonies. The underground hideout is especially useful during wintertime, when they hibernate.

✳ Common hamster

The hamster can scoop up quite an impressive amount of food for winter in its cheeks, which it carries into its underground den.

Eurasian beaver

Lesser Egyptian jerboa

Capybara

Brown rat

✳ Eurasian beaver

Beavers feed on twigs and the phloem—which are like the veins and arteries—of woody plants. They fell small trees by nibbling at the trunks. They also use wood as a material to build dams across water courses.

✳ Lesser Egyptian jerboa

During the day, the jerboa hides from the scorching heat of the African desert underground. It comes out to hunt for food at night, using its long hind legs to make impressive jumps.

✳ Capybara

The capybara, the largest rodent on the planet, lives in South America, near bodies of water. It grazes on both terrestrial and water vegetation. Since it's a good swimmer, it always runs into the water when in danger.

Ungulates

Is one OK? Or would two be better?

A simple structure of the leg, which involves a hoof, gives these large mammals the endurance necessary to travel in search of plants. Depending on the number of their toes, which are protected by a thick horny covering, we divide these animals into even-toed ungulates (such as giraffes) and odd-toed ungulates (horses or rhinoceroses).

Hippopotamus

Wild yak

Markhor

Two-humped camel

Malayan tapir

✷ Wild yak

In rare cases, wild yaks can survive in the inhospitable frozen plains of high mountains. Domesticated yaks, on the other hand, are indispensable helpers to the people of Tibet.

✷ Malayan tapir

Malayan tapirs live in the rainforests of Southeast Asia. It's easy to distinguish them from their cousins, South American tapirs, because the Malayan ones have a white, saddle-shaped stripe.

✷ Red deer

This inhabitant of European forests likes to eat grass. During the rutting season, the males use their antlers to measure their strength against one another. Before winter comes, they shed this adornment.

Hippopotamus

The heavy hippopotamus is an even-toed ungulate—it has four toes on each foot. Hippos love to spend their days in water. Once twilight falls, they go graze on dry land.

Markhor

Markhors are living proof that you can use hoofs to climb rocky terrain like a professional acrobat. The males use their curved horns to fight one another.

Two-humped camel

Camels have two broad, padded toes on their feet, which makes them ideal animals to move around in sand. The two-humped camel comes from Asia.

Black rhinoceros

Plains zebra

Vicuña

Red deer

Black rhinoceros

Black rhinoceroses graze on small bushes and on leaves from tree branches. During the day, they love to roll around in the mud. Tragically, though, frequent poaching has made them an endangered species facing extinction.

Plains zebra

Their body structure and hoof shape make zebras look like their relatives—horses and donkeys. Zebras are odd-toed ungulates who have made their home in African savannas.

Vicuña

This wild llama species lives at high altitudes, where it grazes on grass. Incas used to use its thick coat to weave quality fabrics.

Primates

We're all members of one family.

Monkeys and apes are highly intelligent, due to their favorable brain-to-body-size ratio. Their five-fingered hands are well adapted to grabbing onto branches and other things. Most primates lead social lives and spend a lot of time in trees. Although we humans have stopped using our hands to jump from one tree to another, we're also members of this family. Our closest relatives are chimpanzees.

Golden lion tamarin

Lar gibbon

Philippine tarsier

Chimpanzee

Mandrill

✳ Mandrill

Mandrill males love to show off. Their colorful faces and behinds are impossible to overlook. They look for plants and animals to feed on in tropical rainforests.

✳ Philippine tarsier

Compared to other primates, tarsiers are a tad small. Their remarkably large eyes are very sensitive, allowing them to lead a nocturnal life.

✳ Lowland gorilla

This stocky, muscled gorilla is the largest living primate in the world. Its diet consists mostly of fruits and leaves. Its home is in the dense African rainforests.

✸ Golden lion tamarin

This adorable, intelligent, tiny monkey with a distinct mane feeds mainly on fruits and insects. Its living conditions are being threatened by logging.

✸ Chimpanzee

Social, intelligent chimpanzees live in large groups and tend to help each other. They build nests in tree tops, where they spend the night.

✸ Lar gibbon

Gibbons use their long arms to move hand over hand in a remarkably fast manner. They can safely jump from one branch to another, even if the distance is longer than 30 feet!

Bornean orangutan

Lowland gorilla

Black howler

Hamadryas baboon

11

✸ Black howler

Black howlers excel at two things: their vocalization carries for up to a mile. And to top it off, they are true masters at climbing trees—their long tail is a true help in this regard.

✸ Bornean orangutan

Orangutans tend to be loners who spend most of their time in trees, picking fruit. Their living conditions are being threatened by intensive logging as well.

✸ Hamadryas baboon

Organized baboon packs, led by a male in charge, live in dry grassy regions. They spend most of their lives on the ground.

Predators

No vegetarians over here.

Many predators are feared hunters due to their strong, agile bodies and robust jaws with sharp teeth. Their preferred lunch takes the form of a large chunk of meat. There are exceptions here as well, though. The panda, for example, opts for bamboo, giving steaks a pass.

Brown bear

Grey wolf

Spotted hyena

Lion

Giant panda

12

✳ Grey wolf

Intelligent predators, wolves live and hunt in packs. They even dare to attack prey that's larger than them. Tens of thousands of years ago, when humans and wolves got closer, wolves turned into dogs as a result of breeding.

✳ Giant panda

Even though 99% of its diet consists of bamboo leaves, the extremely rare panda is technically a predator, as it sometimes hunts for small rodents. You can't find it in the wild, with the exception of a few nature reserves in China.

✳ Short-tailed weasel

The small short-tailed weasel is very agile. At night, it likes to go hunting for mice, birds, or rabbits. The northern version has a white fur coat.

Brown bear

The main characteristic features of the brown bear are long claws and a muscled hump. Its diet is rather diverse: it includes both plants and animals, and on occasion honey.

Spotted hyaena

A single hyena doesn't dare attack anything larger than a hare, but a pack of them will easily bring down a zebra. Hyenas look like dogs, but are more closely related to cats.

Lion

Lion males are sturdier than females and rely more on their strength than cunning, which makes them worse hunters. Additionally, they boast a large mane. The females are smaller, but more skilled.

Short-tailed weasel

Amur tiger

Eurasian otter

Walrus

Amur tiger

This mighty yet endangered feline inhabits ever-smaller regions in Asia. The males of the largest tiger species—also called the Siberian tiger—can weigh up to 660 pounds.

Eurasian otter

This predator from the Mustelidae family is well equipped for catching fish. Its thick fur protects it from the cold. It also has webs between its toes.

Walrus

Just like any other pinniped—or seal—the walrus seems a bit clumsy on dry land. But once it gets in the water, it becomes a skilled swimmer that can dive over 300 feet below the surface!

Cetaceans

Is the giraffe my aunt?

It's hard to imagine a giraffe diving in the sea to get food. But believe it or not, giraffes and whales have a lot in common. Both species breathe air, breastfeed their young, and even share a common ancestor. The fact that they're related is also apparent when you compare the whale's fin bones with the bones of this terrestrial even-toed ungulate.

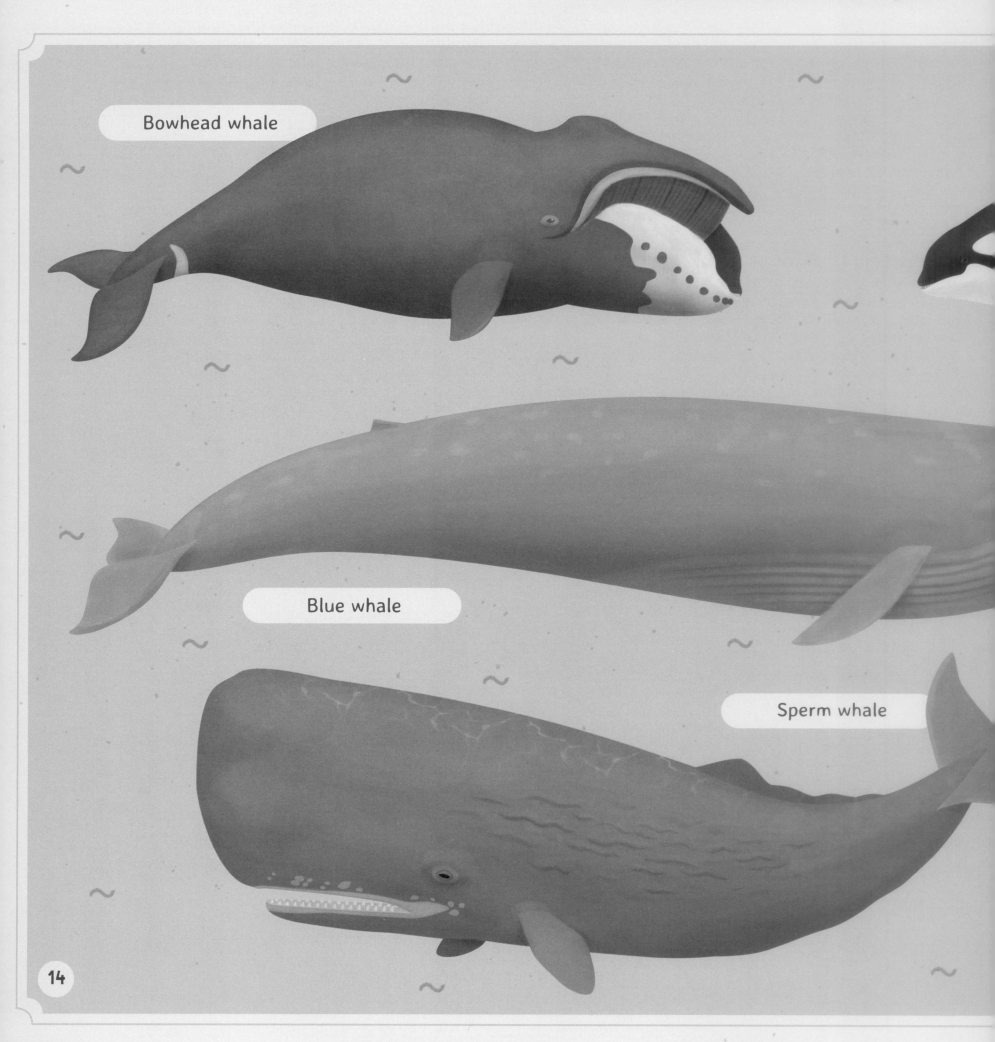

Bowhead whale

Blue whale

Sperm whale

✳ Blue whale

You can find veritable giants among cetaceans. The blue whale, for example, is the largest living animal on Earth. At 200 tons, it's heavier than any dinosaur that ever lived.

✳ Sperm whale

The largest predator in the world dives into the dark, cold depths of the sea to hunt octopuses and giant squids. They can survive for up to two hours without taking a breath, and can dive nearly two miles deep.

✳ Killer whale

Just like dolphins, killer whales are considered toothed cetaceans. They hunt mostly fish, but often go for seals and penguins while in polar regions.

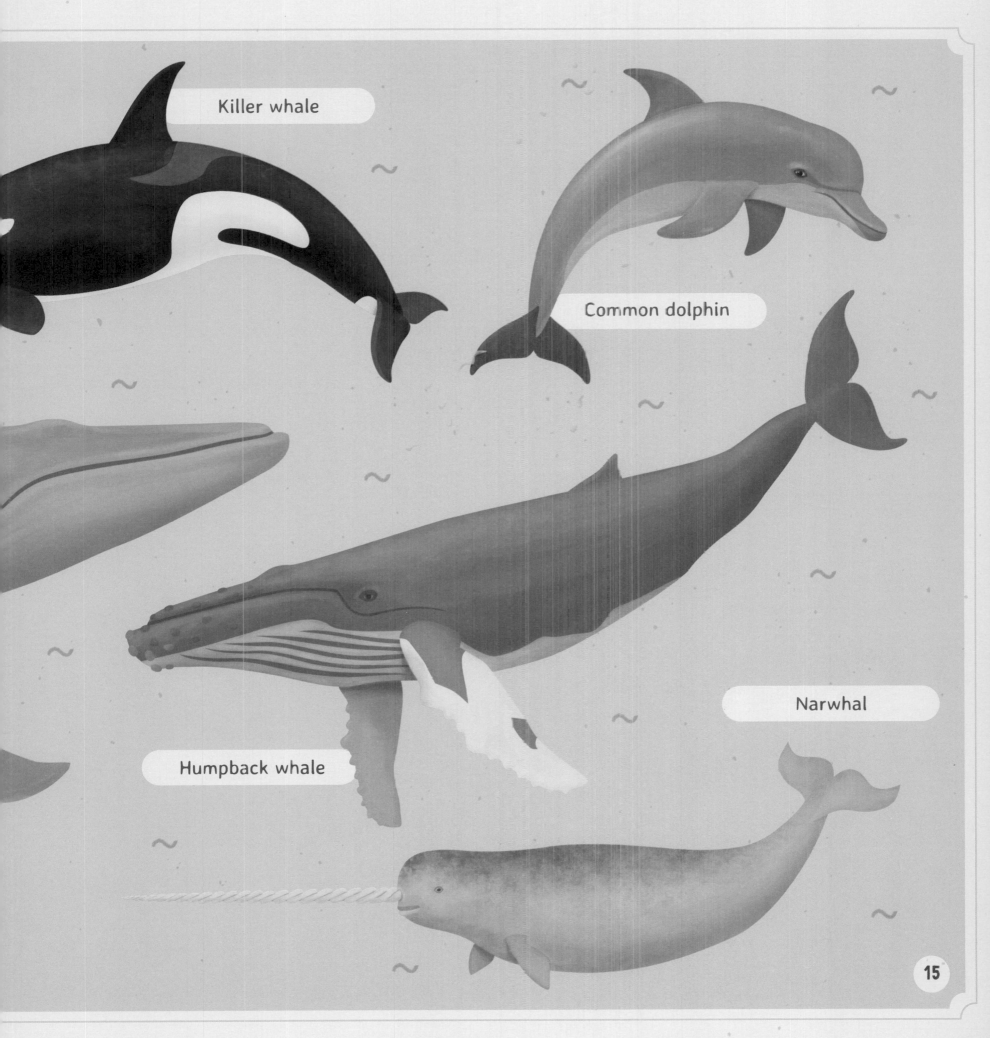

☀ Bowhead whale

The large head of the bowhead whale contains long whalebones whose purpose is to filter tiny organisms out of the water. These whales can live to the respectable old age of 200 years old.

Killer whale

Common dolphin

Narwhal

Humpback whale

☀ Common dolphin

Dolphins are renowned for their extreme intelligence. They lead social lives and communicate by using a wide range of sounds. Each group member has its own name.

☀ Humpback whale

They're also known as whalebone whales. They band together to catch shoals of tiny fish by creating bubble walls. Humpback whales are renowned for their vocalizations.

☀ Narwhal

The head of a narwhal male is adorned by a prolonged tooth that grows from its upper jaw. Narwhals are the northernmost-living mammals in the world.

BIRDS

Apart from feathers and beaks, birds share other characteristic features: they all lay eggs and their forelegs evolved into wings. The bodies of most birds have adapted perfectly to flying. European swifts, for example, are such skilled flyers that they can even sleep while in the air. Those bird species that came to the evolutionary conclusion that flying didn't sit well with them had their wings atrophy. Penguins, for example, use their wings as fins while swimming underwater. Birds use nests to protect their eggs and to hatch them. After hatching, the young are usually featherless, blind, and in need of their parents' care.

Sparkling violetear

The tiny, beautifully colorful violetears are masters of acrobatic flying. They can hover in the air while looking for sweet nectar in blossoms, and can even fly in reverse.

Common ostrich

Ostriches are prevented from flying by their substantial weight. When in danger, they can run at 40 miles per hour due to their strong legs.

Kiwi

The flightless kiwi leads a nocturnal life. It lives in the forests of New Zealand, looking for food by digging in the ground with its long beak.

Sparkling violetear

Toco toucan

Common ostrich

Kiwi

Great horned owl

Peafowl

Toco toucan

Although the distinctly colorful beak of the toucan is light, it's not exactly practical for long flights. It's good for picking fruit from inaccessible twigs and helps regulate body temperature.

Great horned owl

Owls can hunt at night thanks to their sensitive hearing and sharp eyesight. They use their strong legs with sharp claws to catch small animals.

Peafowl

Having a long train isn't exactly practical when you live in the wild. But when it's spread out in a large fan, it's a great tool to attract a mate.

Songbirds

I'm flabbergasted by all this singing.

Most birds can be categorized as songbirds. They use singing to communicate and let others know where they live. Vocalizations can differ rather substantially between individual species. Some species are excellent composers, while others, such as crows, aren't big fans of musical production. Despite their small size, songbirds are very intelligent.

Eurasian bullfinch

Eurasian blue tit

Golden oriole

Bohemian waxwing

✳ Eurasian blackbird

The Eurasian blackbird, sporting a yellow-orange beak, can be frequently encountered in the garden, fighting earthworms. It doesn't say no to insects or berries either.

✳ Bohemian waxwing

A biggish songbird with a small crest atop its head, the Bohemian waxwing often make nests in trees, close to other waxwings.

✳ Northern cardinal

The northern cardinal can be found at the edge of forests and in the gardens of South America. The males have a striking crimson color.

✳ Eurasian bullfinch

Just like other finches, the plump bullfinch has a strong beak—just the thing for cracking open hard seeds.

✳ Golden oriole

The distinctly yellow-and-black orioles most often live in broadleaf forests, where you can hear their typical flute-like singing.

✳ Eurasian blue tit

The beautiful, agile blue tit can often be spotted around human dwellings. It likes to make its home in a nest box so that it can remove insect pests from your garden.

Northern cardinal

European goldfinch

Eurasian blackbird

Song thrush

Barn swallow

19

✳ European goldfinch

Both male and female European goldfinches are known for their wild colors. You can encounter them in European forests and gardens, where they pick seeds.

✳ Barn swallow

Agile swallows hunt insects while flying. They often use pieces of dirt to glue together nests in the walls or beams of houses. Before winter arrives, they leave for warmer regions.

✳ Song thrush

The thrush likes to make nests in open forests. It frequently inhabits gardens, just like its cousin, the blackbird, with whom it shares a similar diet. Thrushes can break snail shells by throwing them against stones.

Parrots

We are vibrant and skilled.

Parrots are renowned for both their beauty and their high intelligence. Their beak and leg shape is well adapted for picking and peeling seeds, nuts, and fruits. Two toes of each of their leg are pointed backwards, providing good support to the bird while it climbs. Parrots are masters at imitating sounds, sometimes even human speech.

Cockatiel

Fischer's lovebird

Scarlet macaw

Rainbow lorikeet

Salmon-crested cockatoo

✸ Salmon-crested cockatoo

The salmon-crested cockatoo is a relatively large bird with a distinct crest. Just like other cockatoo species, this one is very social and playful. When in captivity, it demands a lot of attention and forms a very strong bond with its owner.

✸ Scarlet macaw

The beautiful, rare macaw is the jewel of tropical rainforests and savannas in Central and South America. Their wild colors and big size makes them impossible to miss. They're very social and intelligent.

✸ Budgerigar

In the Australian wilderness, budgerigars often move around in large flocks. The wild budgerigar is exclusively green, but other alternatives of different colors have been successfully bred in captivity.

Cockatiel

This Australian parrot is a favorite pet due to its calm, social disposition.

Fischer's lovebird

The Fischer's lovebird lives in Africa, just like other parrots of the Agapornis genus. It forms smallish flocks in the wild.

Rainbow lorikeet

The Australian rainbow lorikeet looks like it fell into a painter's palette. It loves to feast on fruits grown in orchards and vineyards.

Grey parrot

Budgerigar

Kea

Eastern rosella

Grey parrot

People like to keep this gray-feathered, red-tailed parrot in captivity because of its ability to imitate human speech. It's also known as the African grey.

Eastern rosella

The motley rosella also comes from Australia. The males and females live in pairs and raise their young in nests that are hidden in the hollows of trees.

Kea

This New Zealand–inhabiting bird stands out among other parrots too. The kea is very curious and gobbles up just about anything. It can even tear apart carcasses with its beak.

FISH

Life underwater is very diverse. The number of fish species in the world exceeds the number of terrestrial vertebrate species. Fish can breathe underwater due to their gills. The surface of their bodies is often protected by scales. Movement is made possible by two fins. Fish procreate mostly by laying tiny eggs directly into water. Individual species have adapted to living either in saltwater or fresh water. Only some, such as eels, can spend a part of their life in both environments. The world beneath the water's surface is very diverse, especially around the coral reefs in tropical seas.

✳ Rainbow trout

Trout do well in clean and well-oxygenated cool waters. Some trout species spend part of their life in the sea.

✳ Red-bellied piranha

This freshwater predatory fish has earned a reputation for being a dangerous predator. Thanks to their sharp teeth, a shoal of piranhas can gnaw even large prey clean in a minute.

✳ False clown anemonefish

A well-known small colorful fish, the clown likes to hide among the stinging tentacles of anemones. A thin layer of slime on its skin protects it from getting stung.

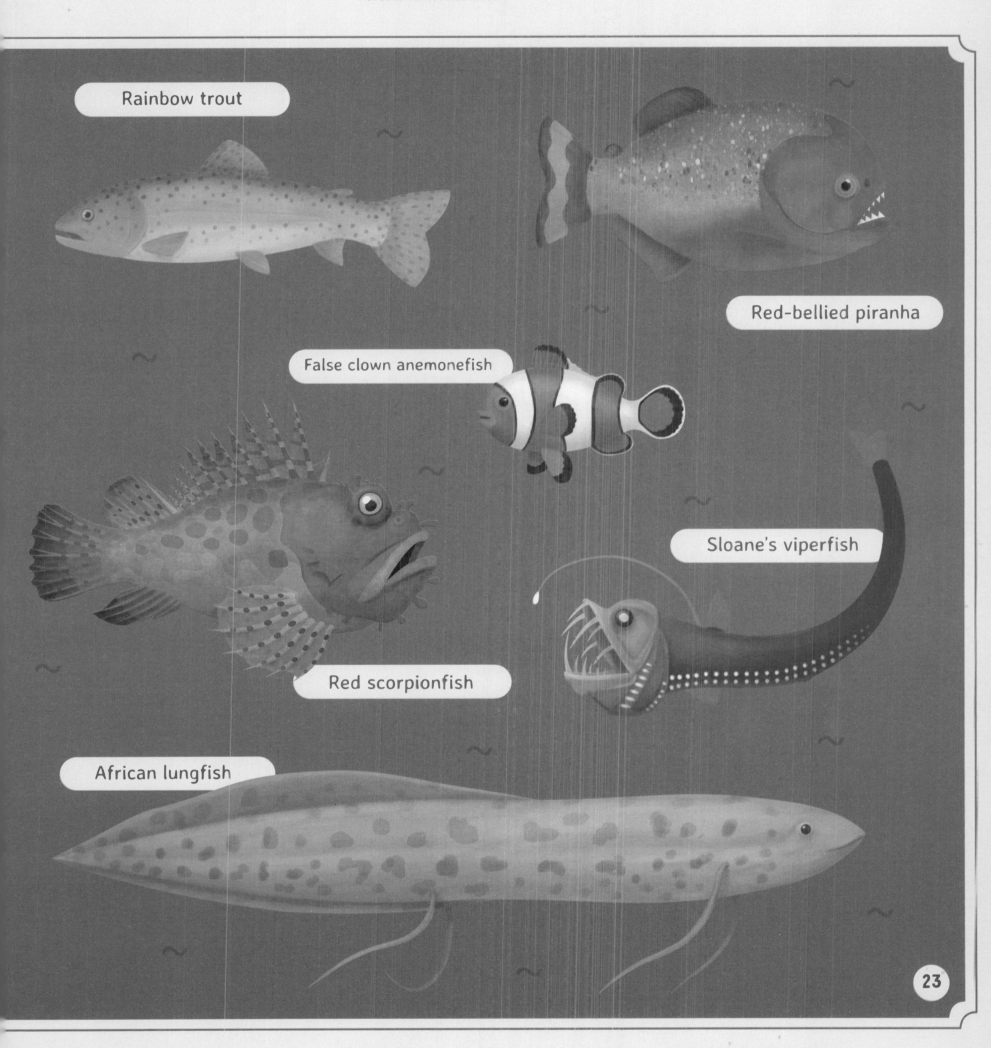

Rainbow trout

Red-bellied piranha

False clown anemonefish

Sloane's viperfish

Red scorpionfish

African lungfish

✳ Red scorpionfish

The well-masked scorpionfish, which lives at the bottom of the sea, can be very dangerous. Stepping on their venomous prickles with a bare foot can be extremely painful.

✳ Sloane's viperfish

All the way down in the deep ocean, where it's completely dark, this luminescent fish lures its prey into its mouth, which is full of long sharp teeth.

✳ African lungfish

Lungfish are unique due to their ability to breathe air. Apart from gills, they're also equipped with pulmonary sacs that allow them to survive dry seasons in mud.

Cartilaginous fish

I have no bones!

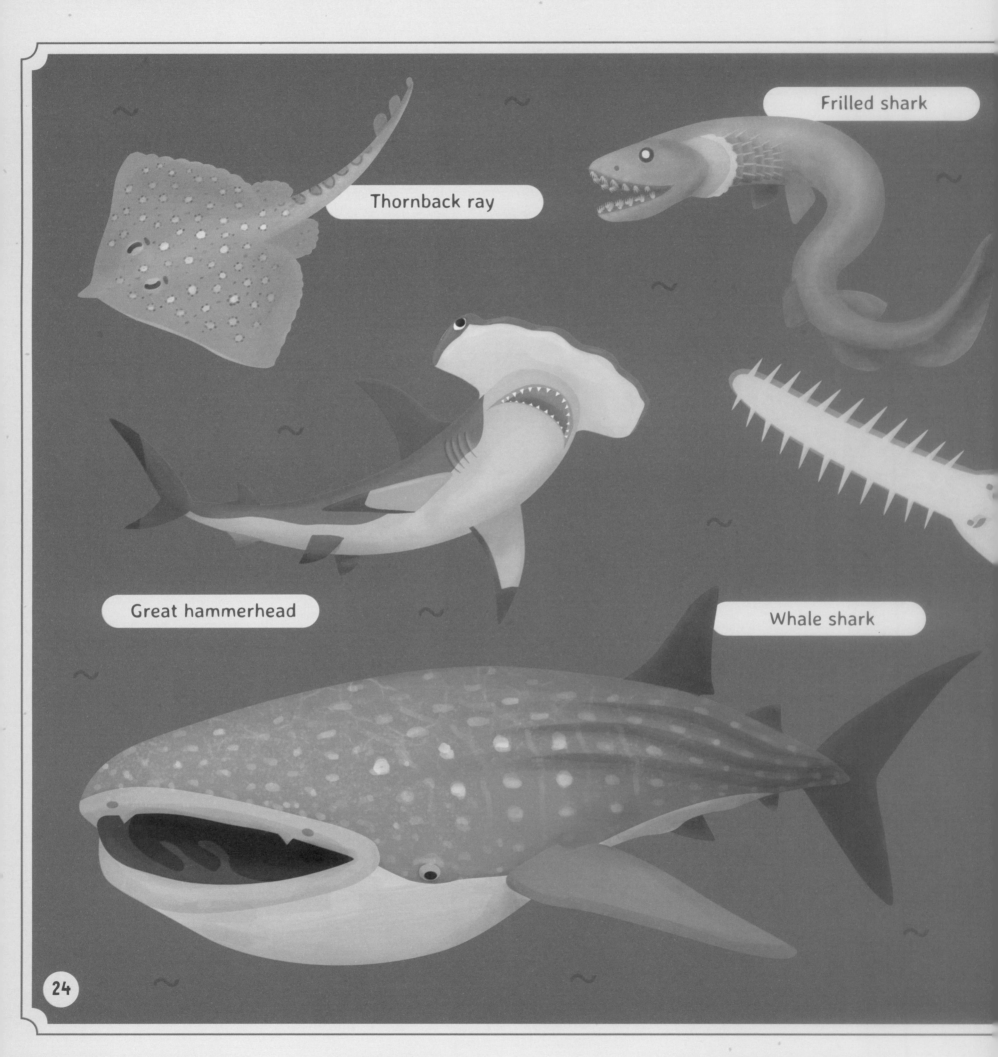

Thornback ray

Frilled shark

Great hammerhead

Whale shark

24

❋ Great hammerhead

This shark can be up to 20 feet long. The unusual shape of its head makes it hard to miss.

❋ Whale shark

Although this is the largest shark in the world, you really don't have to fear it. For food, this calm giant likes to swim around with its mouth open, filtering tiny organisms out of the water.

❋ Smalltooth sawfish

Using a protrusion that is surrounded by teeth on both sides, this fish digs up food from the bottom of the sea, sometimes cutting into a shoal of fish to kill or wound them.

Well-known sea predators, sharks are categorized as cartilaginous fish. This group of animals, equipped with a cartilaginous skeleton, also includes rays and chimaeras. These animals never need to see a dentist because their teeth are constantly replaced with new ones.

Thornback ray

The pattern on the upper part of the ray's body makes it blend in with the bottom of the sea, where it spends most of its time. The thornback ray frequently appears in European coastal waters.

Frilled shark

The frilled shark looks like a species that went extinct long ago. It lives in deep waters. Its gills consist of a single slit, distorted to resemble a collar.

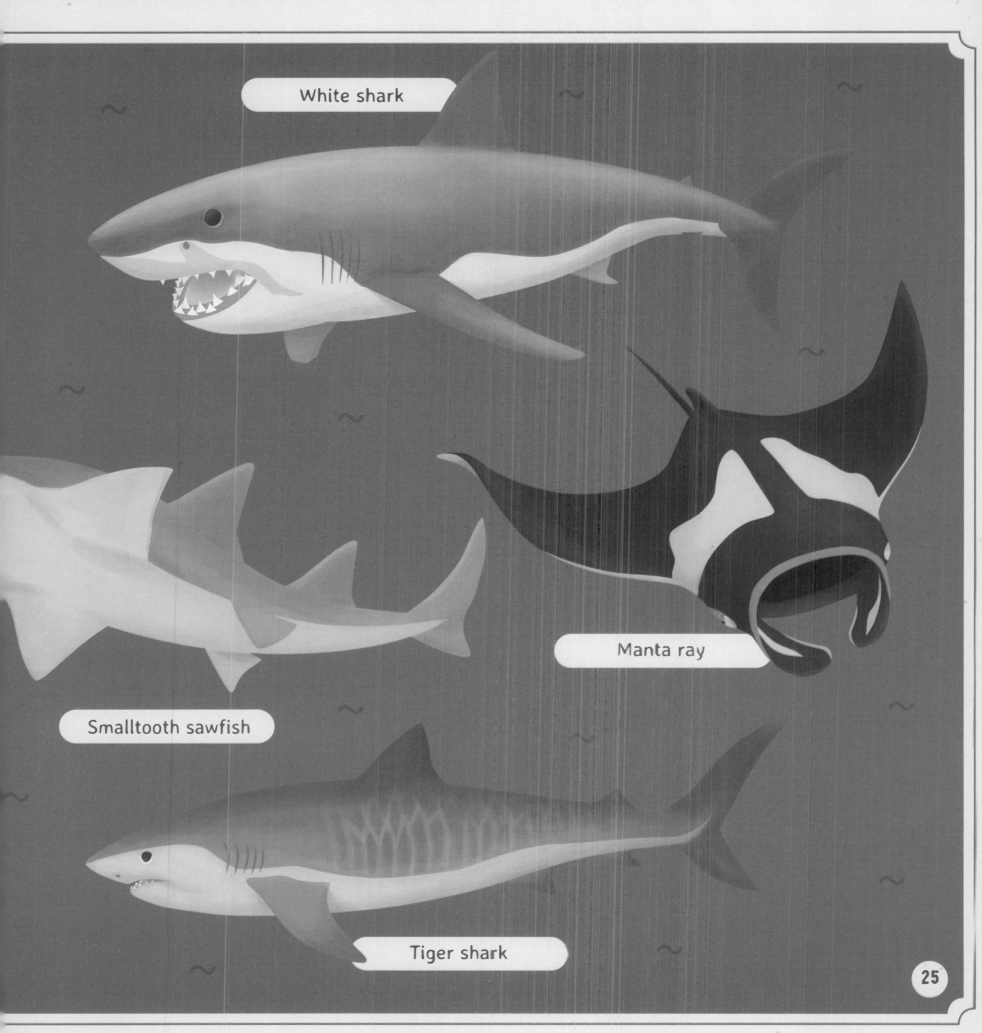

White shark

Smalltooth sawfish

Manta ray

Tiger shark

White shark

Even though the huge, toothy jaws of white sharks scare people half to death, these animals attack people only very rarely. White sharks prefer fish and seals.

Manta ray

The manta's elegant, large, strong fins make it look as if it flies like a bird. Its diet consists of plankton.

Tiger shark

The tiger shark is easily recognizable by the typical stripes on its sides. It's not a picky eater and often sinks its teeth into a carcass. You can encounter it in shallow coastal waters.

AMPHIBIANS

Even though amphibians spend most of their life on dry land, they need water to develop. Most species begin as larvae, are born out of eggs laid in the water, and breathe with gills. The gradual transformation into an animal with limbs and lungs can be observed by studying tadpoles in a pond. The body of an amphibian is covered by smooth skin that excretes slime and toxic secretions. The slime prevents the body's surface from drying out while the venom discourages predators from attacking. The wet skin, filled with blood, allows some species to breathe with the surface of their body.

Mexican axolotl

The axolotl has found the recipe for eternal youth. It's so happy as a larva that its body never transforms into that of an adult terrestrial specimen. The rare axolotls that live in the wild are usually black.

European tree frog

The bright-green tree frogs are renowned for their vocalizations. They croak in the mating season and very often right before it starts raining.

European common frog

The European common frog can be found in large numbers on the European continent. It prefers wet places near water so that it can easily escape predators.

Mexican axolotl

European tree frog

European common frog

Red-eyed treefrog

Poison dart frog

Fire salamander

Red-eyed treefrog

The motley red-eyed treefrog brings water up onto leaves that float on the surface of the pond and lays its eggs there. The hatched tadpoles then fall off the leaves directly into the pond.

Poison dart frog

The dazzling colors of poison dart frogs serve as a warning to prospective attackers. Their skin is covered with lethal venomous secretions.

Fire salamander

The fire salamander most often lives in European mountain forests. Its larvae grow up in small lakes or brooks.

REPTILES

Neither fish nor amphibians, reptiles create their own body heat. They have the same body temperature as the environment they live in. If they want to limber their stiff body up in cold weather, they have to get warm in the sun first. Their body is protected by scaly skin that must be shed regularly. Some snakes have a good sense of smell and sight, which helps them find their way around, as well as other senses for detecting heat. The offspring of tortoises, turtles, crocodiles, and snakes hatch from eggs that were laid on dry land. A few so-called viviparous species come into the world fully developed.

✳ Leopard tortoise

The leopard tortoise is a large African tortoise that eats grass, fruits, and other vegetation that grows in dry bushy and sandy regions. It lays eggs into holes it digs in the ground.

✳ Red-headed agama

This creature looks sort of like a lizard. You can encounter it in Africa, often in the vicinity of houses. The males are distinctly colorful, but only during the day. At night, when they don't have to show off, they turn gray.

✳ Eastern coral snake

Coral snakes hunt lizards, frogs, and other snakes in the warm regions of North America. Unlike the similarly striped king snakes, they're venomous.

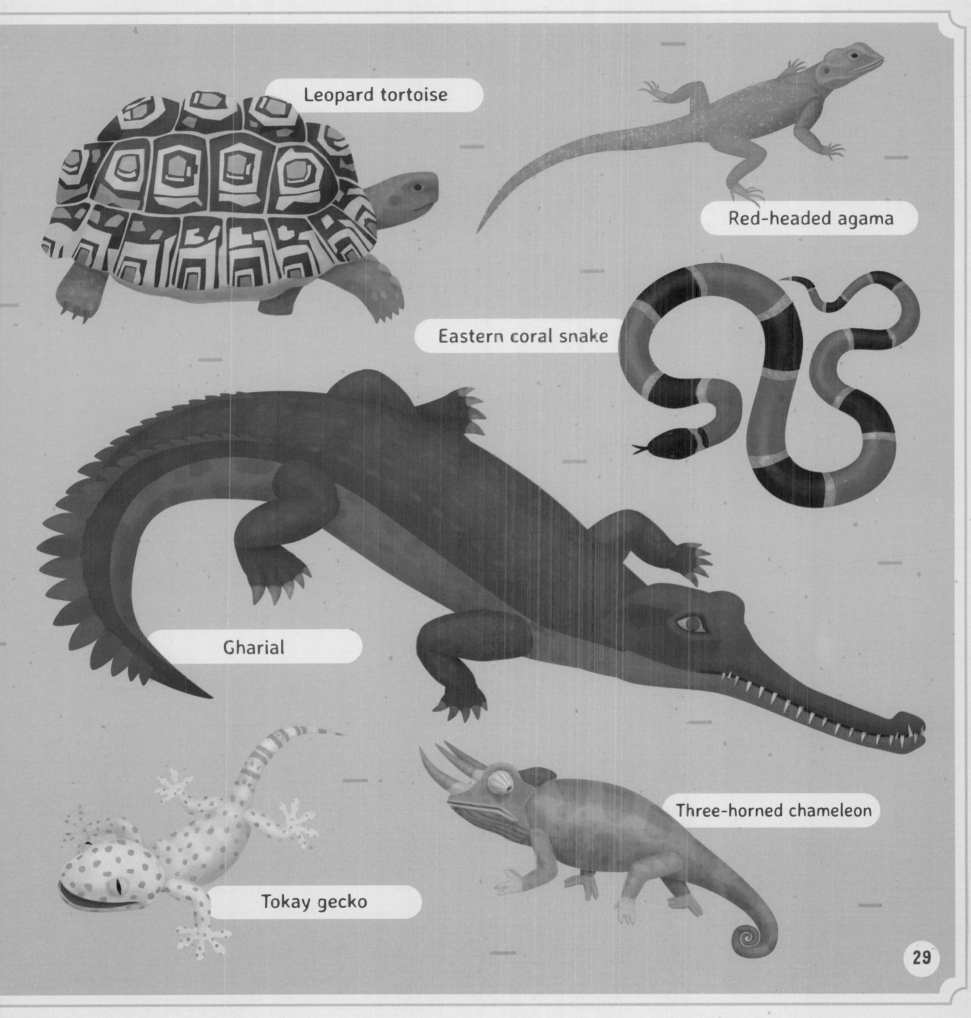

Leopard tortoise

Red-headed agama

Eastern coral snake

Gharial

Tokay gecko

Three-horned chameleon

29

✳ Gharial

The rare gharial has jaws that are ideal for catching fish. It sometimes snaps up water birds too. Its long tail makes it a very skilled swimmer.

✳ Tokay gecko

The broad sticky pads on their toes allow geckos to climb even smooth walls and tree trunks. Tokay geckos are nocturnal animals. The males make a sound that resembles barking.

✳ Three-horned chameleon

The three-horned chameleon, also known as Jackson's chameleon, hunts insects by darting its long sticky tongue out of its mouth. The males use their horns when fighting one another.

Snakes

In my case, legs are not required.

Highly perceptive senses, extreme patience (often in association with excellent camouflage), and frequently also potent venom make snakes highly successful, feared predators. Boa constrictors and pythons wrap their bodies around their prey and gradually suffocate it by squeezing.

Green anaconda

Common garter snake

Royal python

Egg-eating snake

Emerald tree boa

30

✳ Common garter snake

As a grass snake, the common garter snake isn't venomous. It can be found close to bodies of water. Its prey consists mostly of frogs and fish.

✳ Royal python

This smallish python with a pretty pattern on its body lives in Africa. Pythons are egg-laying snakes. The female lays up to eight eggs and then takes care of them.

✳ Rattlesnake

The segmented rattle at the end of the rattlesnake's tail warns all possible intruders that they might get poisoned. When hunting, the rattlesnake bites its prey and then swallows it whole.

Green anaconda

The legends of a ginormous creature that lives in the overgrown water bodies of South America are blood-chilling. The anaconda is the heaviest snake in the world.

Egg-eating snake

The egg-eating snake limits its diet to bird eggs only. After it crams the eggs into its mouth, it swallows their contents and vomits the empty shell out.

Emerald tree boa

Its green body is folded up like a spring on a tree, ready to strike quickly against any unsuspecting prey. The emerald tree boa relies on its eyesight, but can also perceive the body heat of animals.

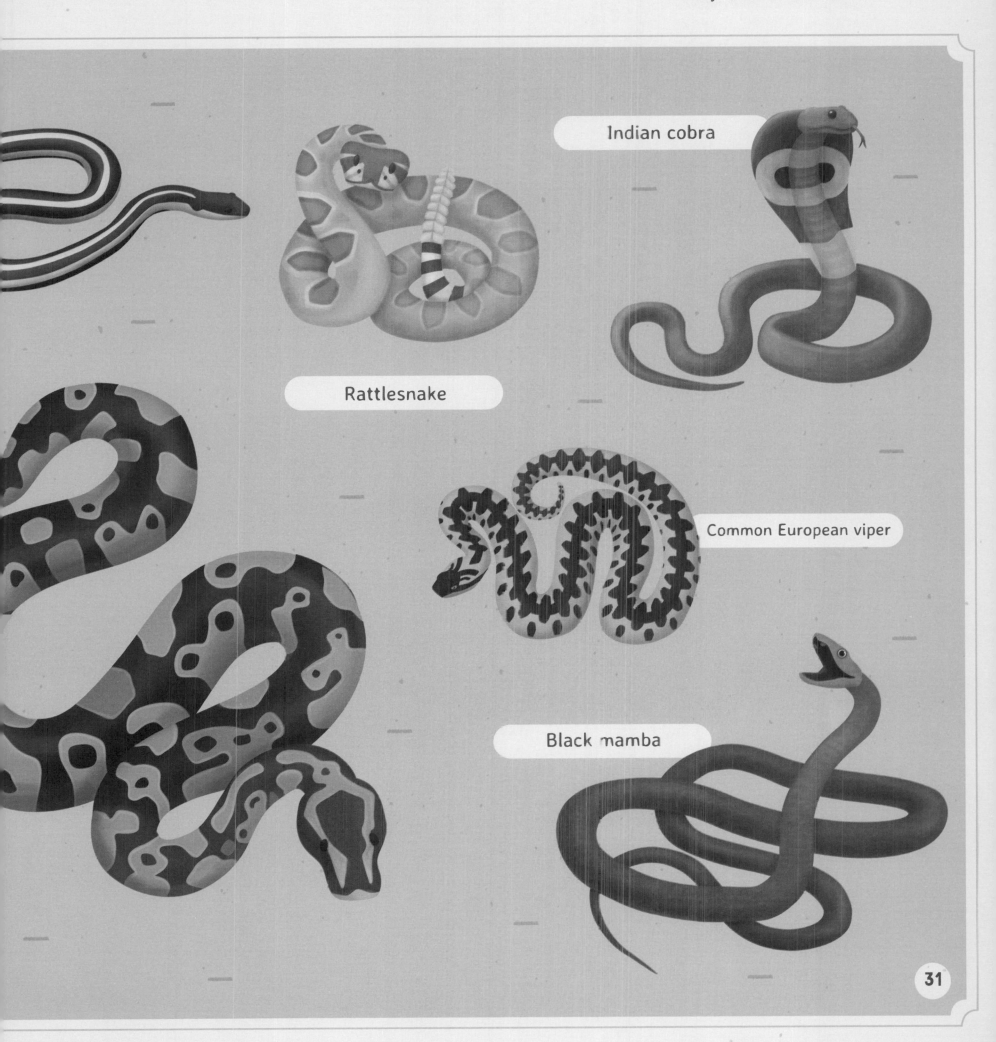

Indian cobra

Rattlesnake

Common European viper

Black mamba

Indian cobra

When the cobra spreads out its neck so that it looks like a cape, it means it feels threatened. Cobras have a pattern on their back that is shaped like a pair of glasses. That's why they're also called spectacled cobras.

Common European viper

This relatively widespread venomous snake can be found in the cold northern and mountainous regions of Europe. It loves to bask in the sun. Its bite is only rarely lethal to humans.

Black mamba

The main weapons of the feared mamba include a potent venom and high speed. It's afraid of people and prefers to get away unless it's directly threatened.

Tortoises

I'm not getting rid of my shell.

The bony shell is directly connected to the body, which is why a tortoise or turtle can never shed it. When in danger, it doesn't have to bother trying to escape (it's bad at escaping, anyway). Instead, the tortoise pulls its head and limbs in, out of the predator's reach. Although tortoises don't have teeth, their sharp jaws allow them to snap off a lot of things, even your finger.

Leatherback turtle

European pond turtle

Galapagos tortoise

Star tortoise

✳ Galapagos tortoise

With a weight of up to 440 pounds, this is one of the largest tortoises in the world. Grazing on vegetation, not hurrying anywhere, and occasionally rolling around in the mud must be a good recipe for long life.

✳ Eastern long-necked turtle

Its exceptionally long neck allows this turtle to walk on the bottom of water currents while occasionally emerging above the surface to take a breath. With a neck like this, it's pretty easy to catch fish too.

✳ Green turtle

The green turtle is well adjusted to long travels across the world's oceans. Just like the leatherback turtle, it lays eggs on sandy beaches.

✻ Leatherback turtle

This noble traveler across the oceans is the largest turtle in the world. Its thin leathery shell is shaped in a way that allows it to move as easily under water as possible. It lays eggs in the holes it digs on a beach.

✻ European pond turtle

The diet of this European freshwater turtle consists of small animals, fish, and insects. The European pond turtle survives cold winters by burying itself in the muddy beds of water courses.

✻ Star tortoise

The terrestrial star tortoise lives in India. Its arched, conical shell with a pretty pattern makes it impossible to miss.

Eastern long-necked turtle

Green turtle

Red-eared slider turtle

Red-footed tortoise

Snapping turtle

✻ Red-eared slider turtle

This freshwater turtle that lives in the water courses and lakes of North America is recognizable by the red stripe on its neck. People like to keep it in captivity.

✻ Red-footed tortoise

About one and a half feet long, this South American tortoise has an elongated shell, decorated with orange spots. Adult specimens prefer to eat plants.

✻ Snapping turtle

The large, predatory, freshwater snapping turtle lives along the Mississippi River. It sometimes lures fish into its very sharp, beak-like jaws by using a worm-resembling protrusion on its tongue.

Lizards

Good thing I'm not a snake.

Snakes have it easy—they lie around all day and the simple shape of their body allows them to shed their skin whole. But being a lizard and having legs is certainly more fun. Slowworms probably don't think so, though—although they're actually lizards, their legs have atrophied.

Panther chameleon

Plumed basilisk

Viviparous lizard

Marine iguana

34

✹ Marine iguana

These large lizards, which live on the coasts of the Galapagos Islands, are surprisingly good divers. They graze on algae. When their body temperature drops too low, they have to come back to the coast to get warmer.

✹ Komodo dragon

This is one truly scary lizard, due not only to its size and appearance but also to its ability to kill large animals. As the largest living lizard, it can lethally wound a buffalo or deer with a single bite of its mouth that's full of venomous teeth.

✹ Thorny devil

This Australian lizard isn't exactly a great runner, which is why it wears a camouflage piece of armor that's shaped like prickles.

Panther chameleon

The relatively large panther chameleons are distinguished by their motley pattern. Their body changes colors depending on the light, temperature, or even the chameleon's mood.

Plumed basilisk

The basilisk can be most often found up in tree branches, lying in wait for small animals. It can be very agile if it needs to, and its strong hind legs allow it to run even on water.

Viviparous lizard

In Europe and Asia, this lizard's habitat extends all the way to the Arctic region. The viviparous lizard can survive hard frosts by falling into the deep winter sleep of hibernation.

Thorny devil

Frilled lizard

Slowworm

Sulawesi lined gliding lizard

Komodo dragon

Slowworm

Slowworms are often miscategorized as snakes due to their appearance. Their eyelids and their ability to shed the end of their tail when attacked prove that they're actually related to lizards.

Frilled lizard

By spreading its collar, the frilled lizard pretends it's larger than it really is, confusing its attackers for a couple of moments before it escapes up a tree.

Sulawesi lined gliding lizard

The long ribs that spread its leathery wings allow the Sulawesi lined gliding lizard—also known as *Draco spilonotus*—to glide among trees. It can easily cover a hundred or more feet by gliding.

INVERTEBRATES

They don't have a spine or a skull that would contain a large brain. Most of them are tiny and easy to miss. But even if you take into account only ants and termites, their combined weight would easily surpass the weight of all the people living on Earth. The world of invertebrates is very diverse and includes many amazing creatures. The very first animals that inhabited our planet, they live both on dry land and in the oceans. The development of many invertebrate species has several stages. For example, the metamorphosis of cocooned caterpillars into adult butterflies is remarkable indeed.

Barrel jellyfish

Jellyfish are primitive animals. Their gelatinous body is shaped like a bell and contains tentacles with stinging cells.

Mole-cricket

This insect resembles a mole, due to its stocky body and forelegs, which were made for digging. Just like a mole, mole-crickets spend most of their life in underground corridors.

Giant squid

That these huge cephalopods really exist has been proven by all the dead bodies that have washed up on shores. The largest specimens can be up to 65 feet long with its tentacles stretched out.

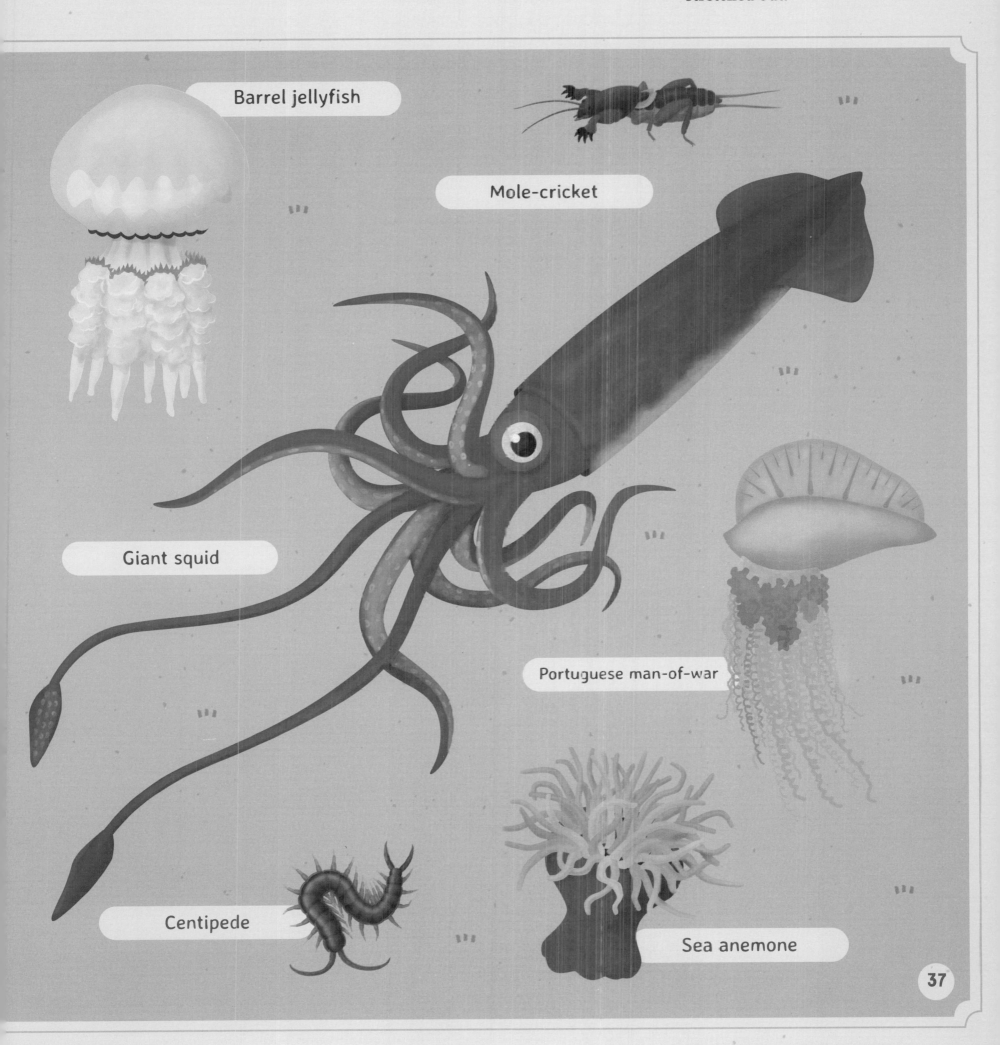

Barrel jellyfish

Mole-cricket

Giant squid

Portuguese man-of-war

Centipede

Sea anemone

Centipede

Centipedes can be up to a foot long. Each segment of their body is equipped with a pair of legs. The first pair has evolved into venomous claws.

Sea anemone

Relatives of corals and jellyfish, anemones lead a settled life. Their strong leg allows them to move only very slowly at the bottom of the sea—so slowly, in fact, that it's imperceptible to the naked eye.

Portuguese man-of-war

This formation consists of a colony of polyps and can be found floating on the water's surface. The inflated bladder has long tentacles that are full of stinging cells.

Arthropods

Our bodies are segmented.

Arthropods include spiders, insects, crabs, and other invertebrate animals whose bodies and legs are segmented and well adapted to their function. The hard body shell serves as an external skeleton and protects the soft internal parts.

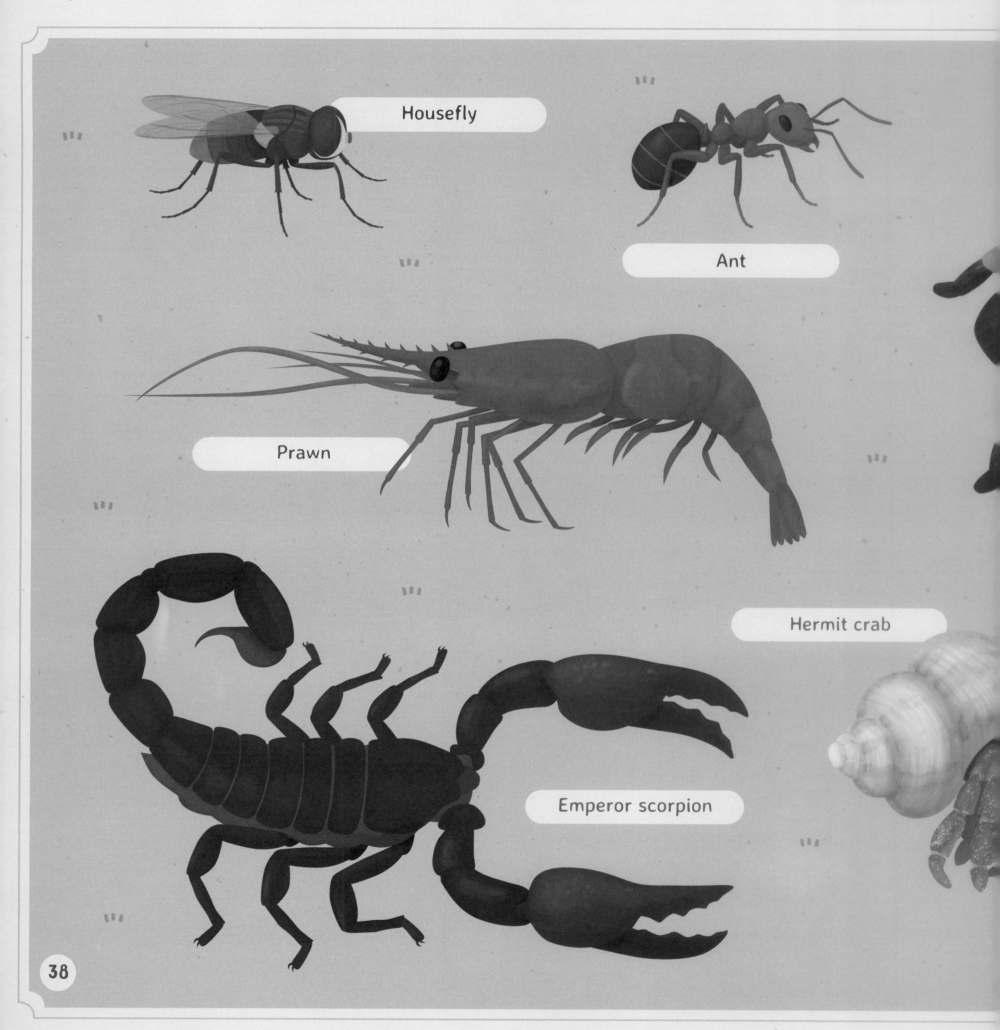

Housefly

Ant

Prawn

Hermit crab

Emperor scorpion

☀ Emperor scorpion

At first glance, this eight-inch-long black scorpion may seem threatening, but it's nowhere near as venomous as some other, smaller species.

☀ Hermit crab

A good accommodation is very important to hermit crabs, as they hide their soft body in a shell they find somewhere. No wonder they often fight one another for the best houses.

☀ Mexican orangeknee

Tarantulas are some of the largest spiders in the world. The beautiful Mexican orangeknee comes from the deserts of Central America. If it's not in a good mood, it sheds hairs that cause irritation.

Housefly

The housefly is a well-known, though not particularly favored, household guest all around the world. Its oral system is adapted to receiving liquid foods. Flies often carry diseases.

Ant

Due to their adaptability, organized character, and diligence, remarkable ants have managed to spread all around the world.

Prawn

Just like other malacostracans—or large crustaceans—the prawn has eye stalks and long feelers. The larvae form a part of sea plankton.

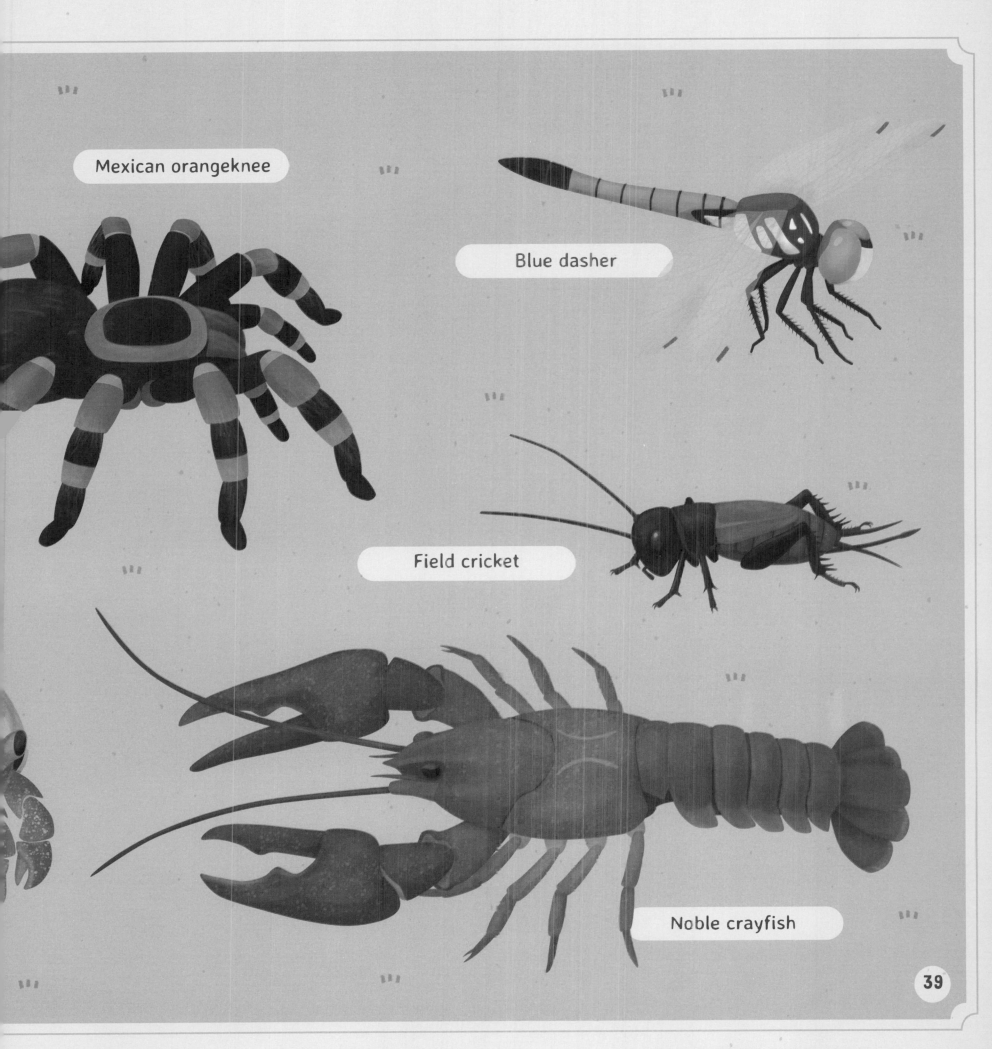

Mexican orangeknee

Blue dasher

Field cricket

Noble crayfish

Blue dasher

Large wings and compound eyes that cover its moving head give dragonflies excellent maneuvering and flying skills. They're born as nymphs that live in water.

Field cricket

Male field crickets announce their presence to the females by loudly vocalizing in a way that sounds like music. The sound is produced when the males rub the tips of their wings together.

Noble crayfish

The noble crayfish used to be abundant in European brooks and rivers, but nowadays they're relatively rare. They hide under rocks and burrow into mud.

Insects

Six legs are enough.

The body of an insect consists of a head, chest, and bottom and is carried around on three pairs of legs. Spiders have a prosoma, a bottom, and eight legs, which is why they're not part of the insect class.

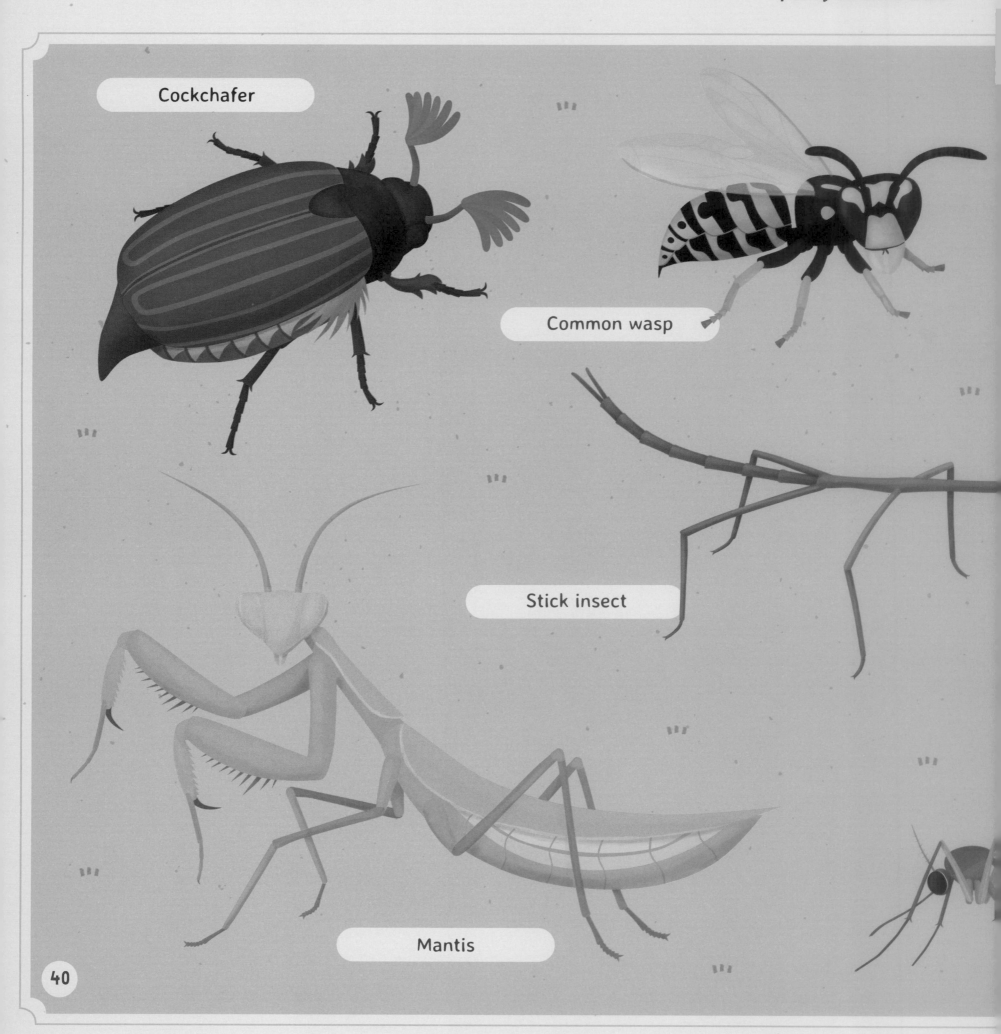

Cockchafer

Common wasp

Stick insect

Mantis

✸ Mantis

This feared hunter relies on its excellent eyesight and strong forelegs. Its triangular head is very flexible. Its eyes are aimed forward, allowing the mantis to accurately evaluate distances.

✸ Mosquito

Most often, we're afraid of tigers or other predators. But there's another danger lurking in the tropical regions—much larger, yet hidden in a much smaller body. Mosquitos can carry life-threatening diseases.

✸ Flea

A plentiful parasite, the flea sucks the blood of its host. Some species target cats, others prefer humans. The skin becomes reddish and itchy as a result of a flea bite.

Cockchafer

Before pesticides started to be used in agriculture, this beetle was so widespread in Europe that it sometimes even appeared in some people's diets.

Common wasp

The wasp may not be particularly well liked because of its sting, but it's useful and it helps fight caterpillars and other pests. Adult wasps feed mainly on nectar.

Stick insect

The bizarre appearance of stick insects has one purpose only—to make it look like a piece of a plant as much as possible. Some stick insects indeed do resemble walking twigs.

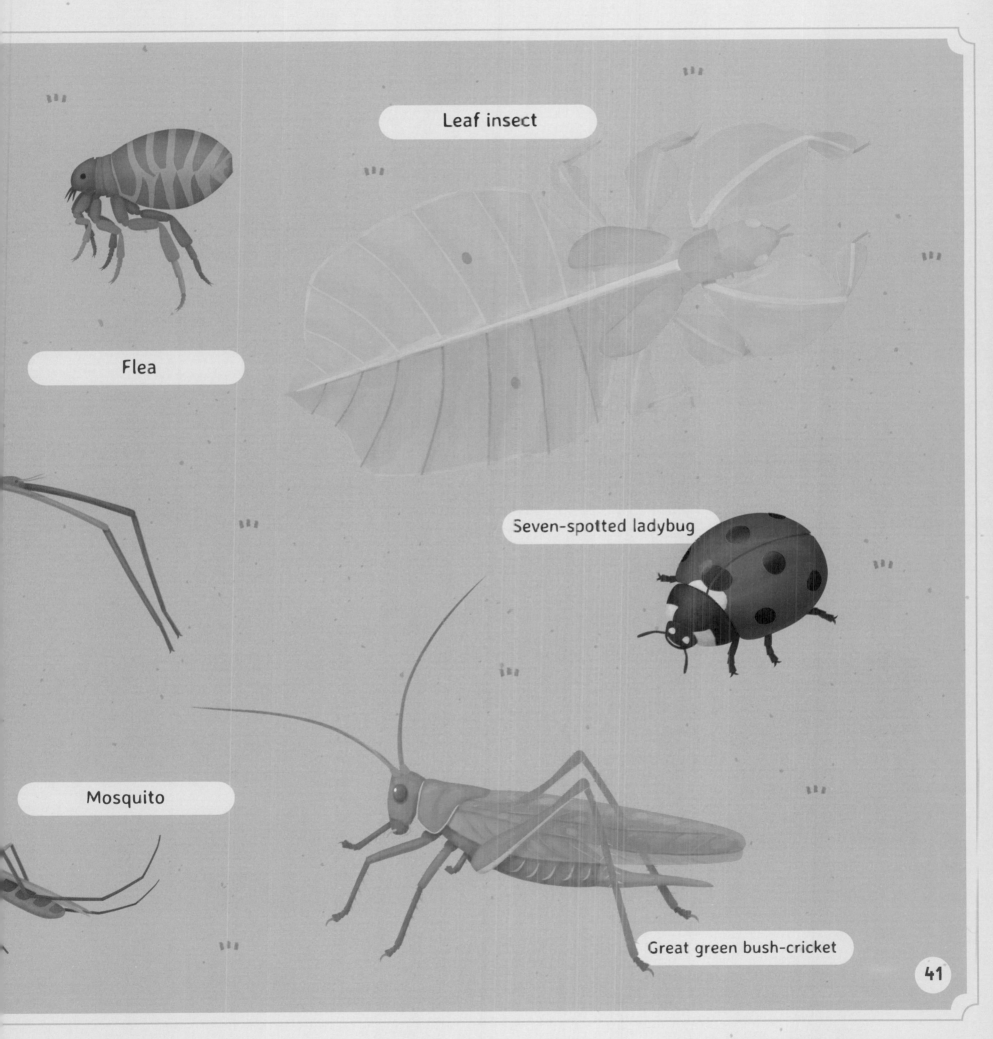

Leaf insect

Flea

Seven-spotted ladybug

Mosquito

Great green bush-cricket

Leaf insect

Leaf insects are masters of turning invisible as well. Their flat broad bottom and the shape of their legs makes them look like leaves.

Seven-spotted ladybug

The useful ladybird helps gardeners fight aphids. If it feels threatened, it excretes a stinking yellow liquid.

Great green bush-cricket

Bush-crickets have distinctly long feelers. You can hear them stridulating (making shrill sounds) at night. Their diet consists mostly of insects.

Beetles

We shield our wings with wing cases.

The membranous wings of insects are thin and fragile. That's why beetles figured out a way to protect themselves. Hard "shards"—casings that cover their wings and back—allow beetles to inspect even narrow spaces without getting themselves in danger.

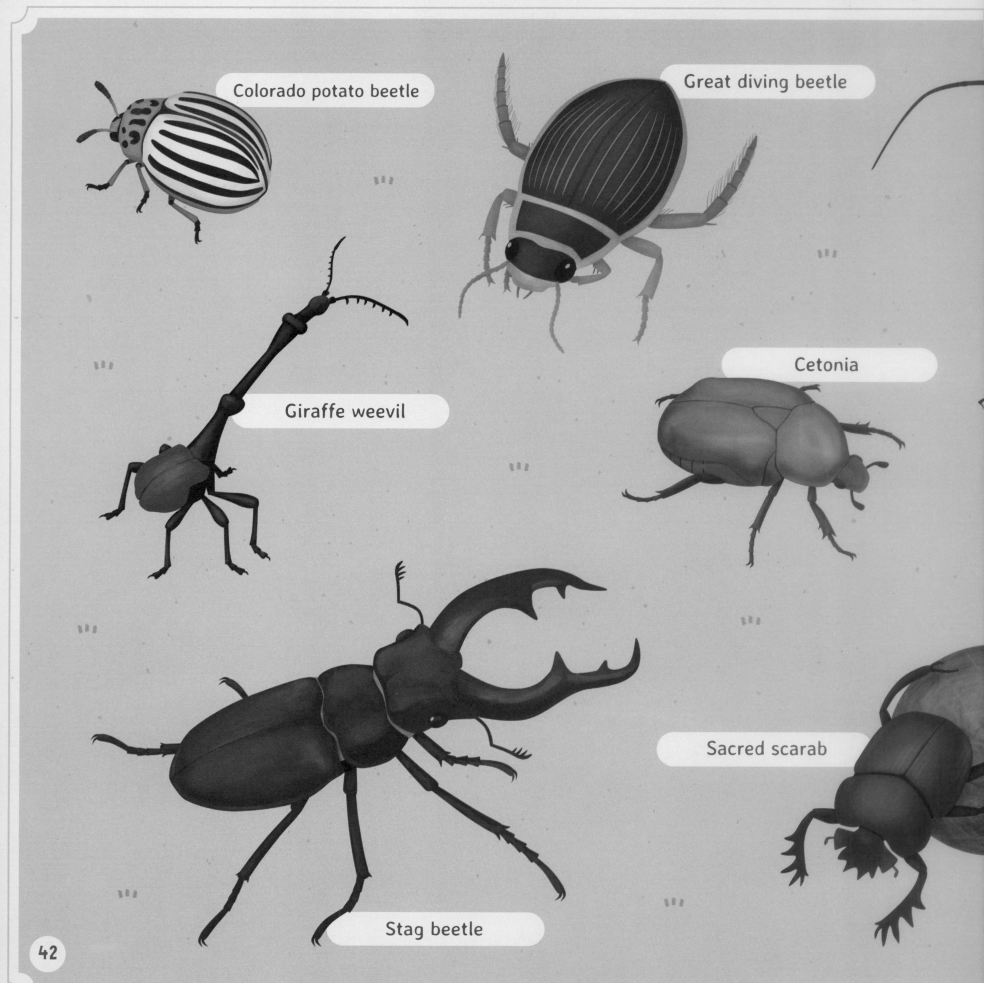

Colorado potato beetle

Great diving beetle

Giraffe weevil

Cetonia

Stag beetle

Sacred scarab

42

✺ Stag beetle

The largest European beetle, the stag beetle, has huge mandibles on its head. The males use them when fighting one another.

✺ Cetonia

The Cetonia genus includes species that look like gemstones or polished metals due to their colorful shiny shards. These shards are closed during flight.

✺ Sacred scarab

As the name suggests, the sacred scarab was considered sacred in Ancient Egypt. The greatest treasure it owns is a ball of dung it knocks together and then rolls to a place that's suitable for laying eggs.

❋ Colorado potato beetle

This well-known beetle has a distinct striping on its shards. It feeds on potato haulms. Gradually, the Colorado potato beetle has spread from America to Europe and Asia.

❋ Great diving beetle

The great diving beetle dives into ponds to get food. It also hunts insects and other small animals. While diving, it has a supply of oxygen hidden beneath its shards, similarly to human divers.

❋ Giraffe weevil

The giraffe weevil uses its long neck to build a nest from leaves and to engage in fights. It can be found only on the island of Madagascar.

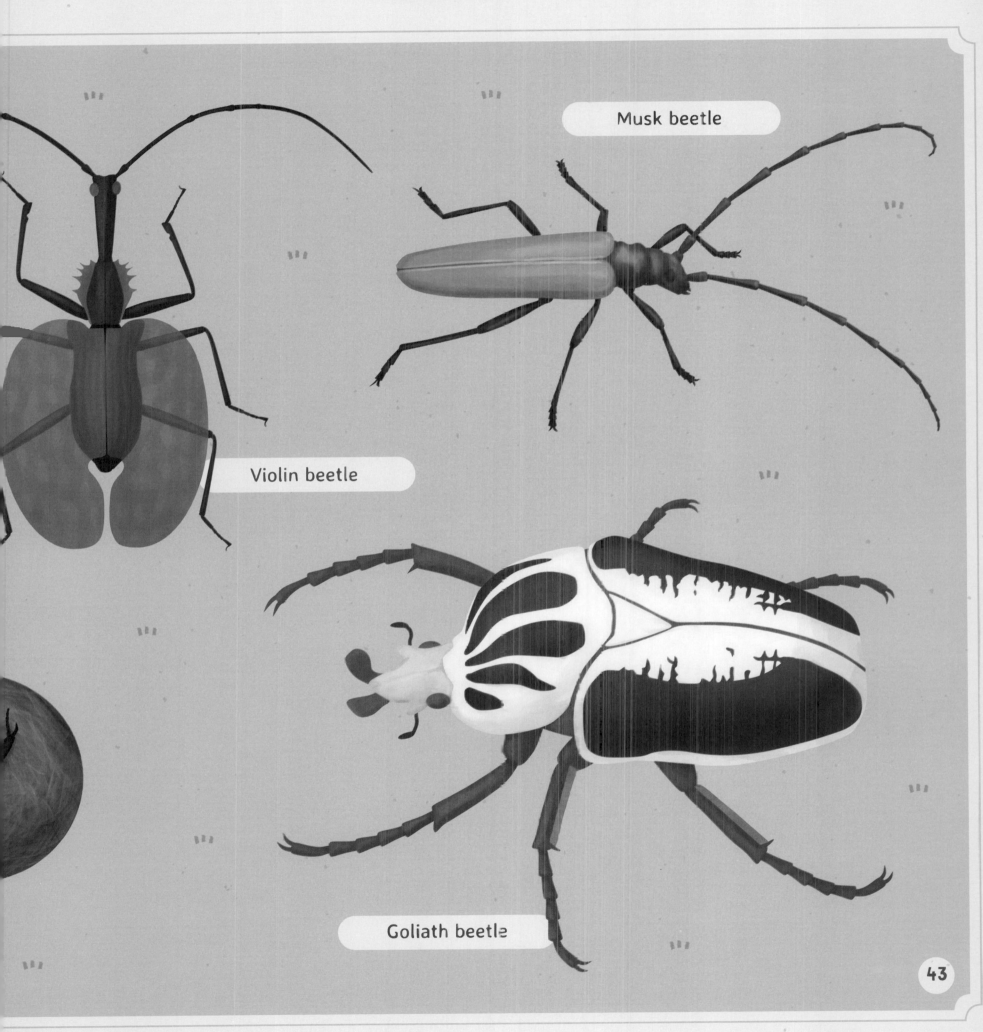

Musk beetle

Violin beetle

Goliath beetle

43

❋ Violin beetle

Ground beetles boast some remarkable specimens as well. As the name suggests, the violin beetle, which can be found in the tropical rainforests of Southeast Asia, looks like a violin due to the shape of its body.

❋ Musk beetle

The adult musk beetles gather pollen from flowers or suck nectar and sap from plants. The larvae—well-known wood pests—hatch from eggs laid under tree bark.

❋ Goliath beetle

One of the largest beetles in the world, Goliath beetles live in the equatorial rainforests of Africa. Their larvae live in rotting wood and are remarkably large as well.

Butterflies

We have dazzling wings.

Caterpillars usually aren't very interesting. No wonder, then, that they want to show off their beautiful wings immediately after they turn into an adult butterfly. Butterflies have a proboscis—an elongated mouthpart—whose purpose is to help them suck sweet nectar. It's curled until the butterfly settles on a blossom and tastes the blossom's flavor with its feet.

Silkworm moth

Monarch butterfly

Atlas moth

Cabbage white

Peacock butterfly

44

✳ Peacock butterfly

The colorful eyespots on butterfly wings can look like the eyes of large animals to some attackers and dissuade them from attacking. The black caterpillars of this beautiful peacock butterfly can be found on nettles.

✳ Monarch butterfly

Related to the Nymphalidae family, the monarch butterfly is a record-holder in covering long distances—it can cover thousands of miles as part of its yearly migration.

✳ Ornithoptera priamus

The male of Ornithoptera priamus is a large tropical butterfly with a distinct green-and-black pattern. The females of this species have a much less noticeable colorful pattern.

Silkworm moth

This nocturnal butterfly has been bred by people for several thousands of years. The fibers of cocoons that contain larvae are used to make silk and weave delicate fabrics.

Atlas moth

The atlas moth has the largest wing surface of any insect. It has a wingspan of nearly a foot long.

Cabbage white

You can frequently encounter cabbage whites in agricultural regions. The female often lays its eggs on cabbage leaves and other kinds of vegetables.

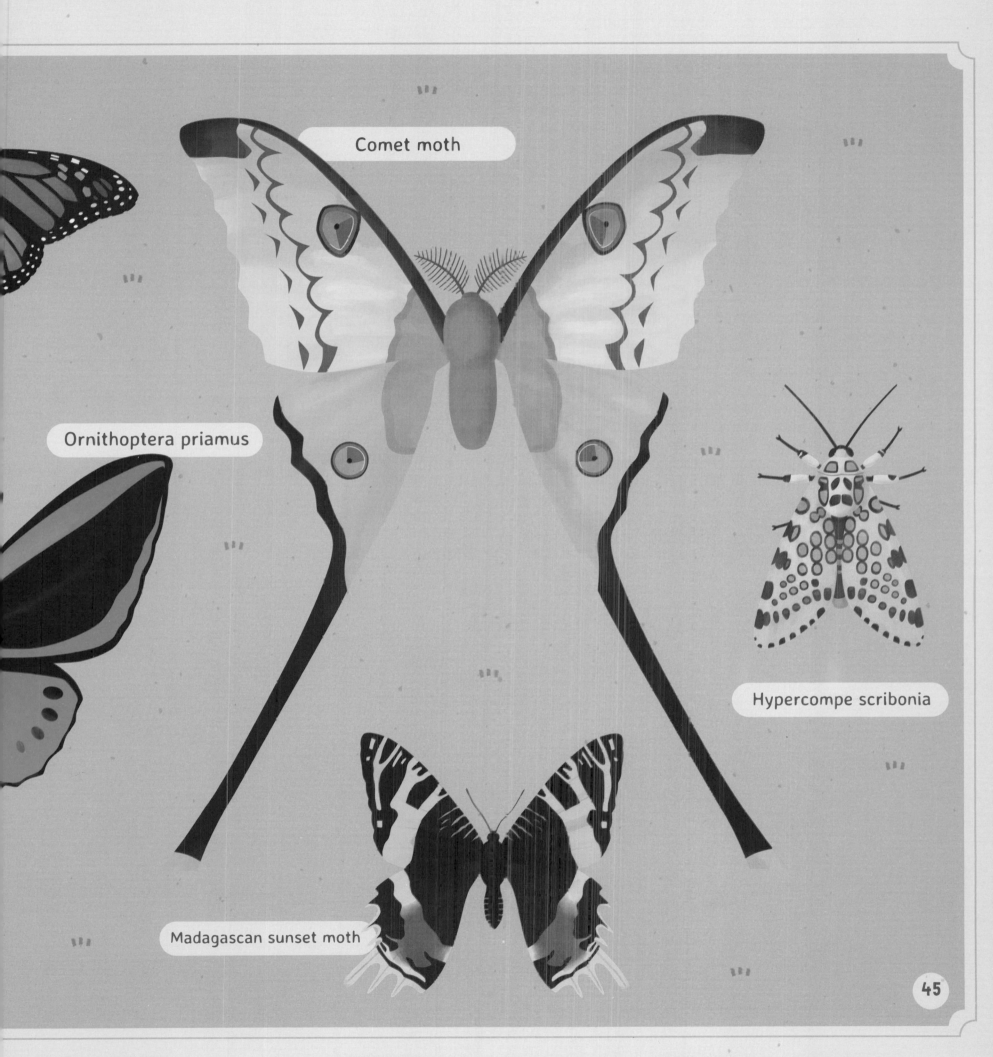

Comet moth

Ornithoptera priamus

Hypercompe scribonia

Madagascan sunset moth

45

Comet moth

One of the largest butterflies on Earth, similarly to the Atlas moth, which it's related to. The wings of the comet moth are adorned with long spurs that are impossible to overlook.

Madagascan sunset moth

The motley sunset moth lives in forests on the island of Madagascar. Its shiny colors aren't created by pigments but by a microscopic structure on the surface of their wings that reflects light.

Hypercompe scribonia

Hypercompe scribonia is active at night. Nocturnal butterflies are known for having only muted colors. They navigate their way around by relying on scent, not sight.

Mollusks

Welcome to my home—my shell.

The bodies of mollusks are protected by calcic shells. Octopuses, though, don't need any heavy casing—they have good senses and are masters at finding shelters. The double shell of mollusks like oysters is called a bivalve shell. The house of gastropods, such as snails, is known simply as a shell.

Giant clam

Roman snail

Chambered nautilus

Common cockle

46

✴ Common cockle

The cockle's bivalve shell consists of two ribbed shells that are equal in size. Cockles play a big role in the food industry.

✴ Blue-ringed octopus

The blue rings on its body serve as a warning that this smallish octopus shouldn't be touched. Its bite is venomous enough to kill even a grown man.

✴ Great grey slug

The grey slug is approximately six inches long. Active mostly at night, it gobbles up a large amount of plants but also won't say no to small gastropods.

Giant clam

Weighing over 440 pounds, the giant clam is one of the largest living bivalves in the world. It can be found in the shallow, warm waters of coral reefs.

Roman snail

Unlike sea gastropods, the terrestrial ones have a light, thin shell. They like to take walks around the garden while it rains.

Chambered nautilus

The Nautilus family includes the only cephalopods in the world with external shells. The chambered nautilus has been living on Earth for over 500 million years, which is why it's called a "living fossil."

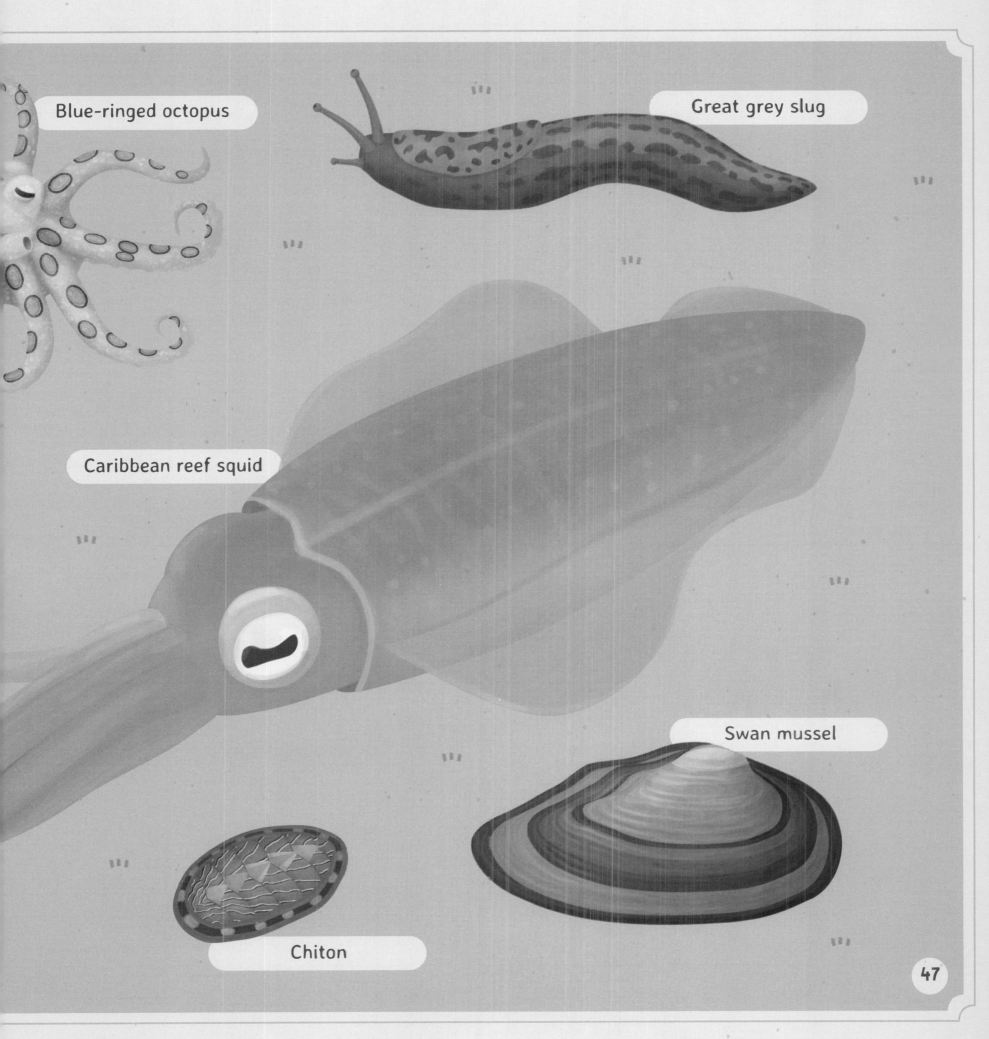

Blue-ringed octopus

Great grey slug

Caribbean reef squid

Swan mussel

Chiton

Caribbean reef squid

The Caribbean reef squid moves around by waving the fins on its sides. It can quickly change the color of its body. These visual effects are used for communication as well.

Chiton

The chiton's adhesive leg is protected by eight overlapping plates. It lives in sea bays on rocks and stones.

Swan mussel

Most bivalve species live in the sea. However, the swan mussel is a freshwater species. It can be found at the muddy bottoms of ponds or in the still waters of river inlets.

Encyclopedia
of Animals
for Young Readers

Written by Tomáš Tůma
Illustrated by Tomáš Tůma

© B4U Publishing for Albatros,
an imprint of Albatros Media Group, 2022
5. května 1746/22, Prague 4, Czech Republic
Printed in China
by Dongguan Eastcolor Paper Products Co.,Ltd

www.albatrosbooks.com

ISBN: 978-80-00-06352-2